DURHAM – THE GREAT CITY

DURHAM
THE GREAT CITY

PHILIP NIXON

HALSGROVE

First published in Great Britain in 2014

Copyright © 2014 text and photographs Philip Nixon
A number of images from this book were originally published in Philip Nixon's *Portrait of Durham* in 2006

Title page: Durham Cathedral, the Old Fulling Mill and The River Wear.

British Library Cataloguing-in-Publication Data
A CIP record for this title is available from the British Library

ISBN 978 0 85704 206 4

HALSGROVE
Halsgrove House,
Ryelands Business Park,
Bagley Road, Wellington, Somerset TA21 9PZ
Tel: 01823 653777   Fax: 01823 216796
email: sales@halsgrove.com

Part of the Halsgrove group of companies
Information on all Halsgrove titles is available at: www.halsgrove.com

Printed and bound in China by Everbest Printing Co Ltd

Victorian terraced houses typical of the
city huddle together near the viaduct –
as seen from Wharton Park.

Introduction

Over the years many excellent comments have been made about the ancient City of Durham. No doubt its charm lies in the breadth of its great variety – it is a subtle blend of sylvan riverside scenery, shaded pathways, singularly attractive buildings of varied architectural styles, wonderful bridges, rich industrial heritage, historic schools and colleges, a busy market place, quiet parks and old cobbled streets, all woven into a rich and colourful tapestry around the much loved World Heritage Site of the Castle and Cathedral which, in turn, presents a skyline that is perhaps unequalled anywhere in the world. All this is enriched by a vibrant mixture of lively people who proudly live, learn, work and visit this exciting, fascinating, charming, romantic almost mystical historical place.

As well as in daylight Durham also weaves its own kind of magic after dark. The city takes on a different look and feel; the ancient floodlit buildings look completely different and a whole new range of patterns, shadows and colours come into being. Even the residual light spill provides interesting illumination and what may have been mundane subjects in daylight suddenly become striking and sometimes even sinister objects of observation. The floodlit Castle and Cathedral is an unforgettable sight when approaching the city from Leazes Road and the A1 motorway. Floodlighting the Cathedral and Castle was an idea started in the mid sixties by Norman Richardson, businessman, Alderman, former Mayor of the City and honorary Freeman of the City, and how it has progressed: Durham now has the exciting Lumiere Festival – the first was held early in 2010 and was a four-night display of light and music in the city. Among its highlights was Crown of Light, a combination of light and music that saw huge images from the pages of the Lindisfarne Gospels rolling over the front of Durham Cathedral. Over 50 000 people visited the festival which included work by more than 50 artists.

However, Durham's early rise to fame centred upon the ancient

Kingdom of Northumbria's role as the Cradle of Christianity. And so to understand its early beginnings we have to go back to AD634 and the Battle of Heavenfield. It was here, in the shadow of Hadrian's Wall, that King Oswald defeated the pagan hoards of Cadwallon to re-establish a foothold for Christianity in Northumbria. Oswald sent to Iona for missionaries but, we are told in the writings of the Venerable Bede, that the first monks who came *"were beaten by the intractable nature of the people they had come to teach!"* They were soon replaced by the wise and gentle Aidan who, with the help of King Oswald, established a monastery on the Holy Island of Lindisfarne. The importance of this small island grew as the religious teachings spread throughout the north and this it became known as "The Cradle of Christianity".

About the time of the Battle of Heavenfield a boy was born in the Border Hills who was to play a major part in the spread of Christianity and also in the founding of Durham City. His name was Cuthbert.

When he was a young man tending flocks of sheep in the Border Hills he had a vision of a soul being carried to Heaven by a host of angels – he later learned that this took place at exactly the same time as Aidan had died at Bamburgh. Profoundly moved, Cuthbert set off immediately to join the religious community at Melrose and went on to become a highly respected missionary and religious leader. He eventually became Bishop of Lindisfarne after spending ten years as a hermit on the Farne Islands. He died on Inner Farne on 20 March 687 AD and he was buried in the church on Lindisfarne. On his deathbed Cuthbert warned the monks of Viking invasion and told them that, should the need arise, they should exhume his body and flee, rather than let it fall into the hands of the heathens.

Eleven years after his death his body was found to be uncorrupted and it was this event that incontestably decided his worthiness to be a saint. Word of this miracle spread far and wide and a steady stream of pilgrims visited his shrine over the following years. In 875AD the Vikings intensified their raids on the Northumbrian coast, launching a particularly vicious attack on Lindisfarne. The monks, remembering Cuthbert's deathbed warning, fled under the leadership of Bishop Alduhn, and took St Cuthbert's body with them, together with the bones of other northern saints and the head of King Oswald. The Lindisfarne Gospels and other illuminated manuscripts were also placed in an elaborate oak casket. They wandered for eight years and eventually settled in Chester-le-Street, an old Roman settlement, where they stayed for 113 years. However peace did not last and the Vikings raided again and this time the monks took the coffin of St Cuthbert to Ripon. When the danger had passed they set off once again to return north.

Unfortunately the procession was prevented from reaching Chester-le-Street. The cart carrying the coffin stopped fast and could not be moved in spite of much effort. The monks fasted and prayed for three days and St Cuthbert appeared in a vision. He told one of the brethren, Eadmer, that he wished his body to be taken to *"Dunholm-The Hill Island"* but the monks were greatly upset – none of them knew where this was – until, as fate would have it, one of the monks overheard two dairy maids talking. One of them had lost a cow and the other told her it had wandered on to the Dunholm. The monks were delighted and guided by the maids they moved St Cuthbert's body on to this easily defendable natural peninsula. They quickly constructed a shelter made of boughs to protect the precious burden they had carried for so long, and then they knelt solemnly in prayer to give thanks because they had at last, in 995AD, found the final resting place for St Cuthbert.

A relief panel high on the wall of one of the turrets of the Chapel of the Nine Altars of the Cathedral commemorates this event, although some historians believe that this story is a reflection on an old proverb about the later wealth of Durham: *"The Dun Cow's milk makes the Prebends' wives go all in silk".* The earliest documentation of the story dates from the sixteenth century, but whatever the truth the story of the Dun Cow adds and interesting degree of romantic mysticism to the wonderful story of St Cuthbert.

The monks' rough shelter of boughs was soon replaced by a simple wooden church, but even this did not last and in 998AD a stone church, known as the White Church was dedicated and the Saint's body laid within. Pilgrims continued to flock to the shrine of St Cuthbert and the "Community of St Cuthbert" grew. The secular priests with their wives and families lived separately from the church alongside lay brethren and associated tradespeople. Durham grew and prospered and because of continued associated miracles the cult of Saint Cuthbert grew to be greater than that of any English saint at that time, in fact right up to the martyrdom of Thomas Beckett. At the Conquest, William the Conqueror established the principle of the Prince Bishops, to better repel the savage incursions of the Scottish Borderers and to check the Saxon influence in the north.

These Prince Bishops were among the most powerful men in the land, next to the King, and enjoyed all the privileges of royalty within the Palatinate. They had their own parliament, minted their own coins, passed their own laws, raised their own armies, granted charters, enjoyed the right of wreck along the Durham coast together with any whales or sturgeons that were caught – even the King found it necessary to have the Bishop's permission to enter the Palatinate.

The first Prince Bishop, Walcher of Lorraine, proposed to eject the Community of St Cuthbert from Durham but before he could implement any changes he was murdered by a mob at Gateshead because they thought he was involved in the slaying of Lyulph, a Saxon patriot. William the Conqueror did not take this kindly and retaliated with a campaign that became known as "The Harrying of the North" – by 1081 his soldiers had totally devastated the area.

William de St Carileph was next appointed Bishop and it was he who removed the Community of St Cuthbert and brought in his Benedictine Monks. He ordered the building of the mighty Cathedral and on 11 August 1093 the foundation stone was laid. The Castle at Durham is just as imposing as the Cathedral – building began in 1072 by Waltheof, Earl of Northumberland, at the direct order of William the Conqueror. However it is certain that there were earlier defensive works on the site when it was successfully defended against the Scottish King Malcolm in 1006 and in 1036, again against the Scots, this time under King Duncan.

Today the Castle serves as University College but until the death of William van Mildert, the last Prince Bishop from the time of Walcher of Lorraine, it was the home of, or under the tenure of, 50 Prince Bishops. It was in July 1831 that Bishop van Mildert, the Dean and Chapter and a few supporters proposed the creation of a university in Durham and on 4 July 1832 royal support was given to the Bill for the establishment of the University of Durham.

The City continued to grow and today its Cathedral is still the epicentre of religion in the north and probably will continue to be so well into the next millennium.

Philip Nixon

Saddler Street in the festive season

Acknowledgements

Many thanks to all those people who offered invaluable help, advice and support while I was preparing this book:

Valerie Nixon, Mark Nixon, Sophy Nixon, Denis Dunlop, John Stephenson, David Watson MBE, Professor Maurice Tucker and, of course, Simon Butler of Halsgrove for offering me the opportunity.

Particular thanks to Mark for taking the photographs from the top of the central tower of Durham Cathedral and to Archie the Labrador for his company on most of the walks!

Durham Cathedral is the centrepiece of a World Heritage Site. Residents are justly proud of this great distinction granted by UNESCO in 1987.

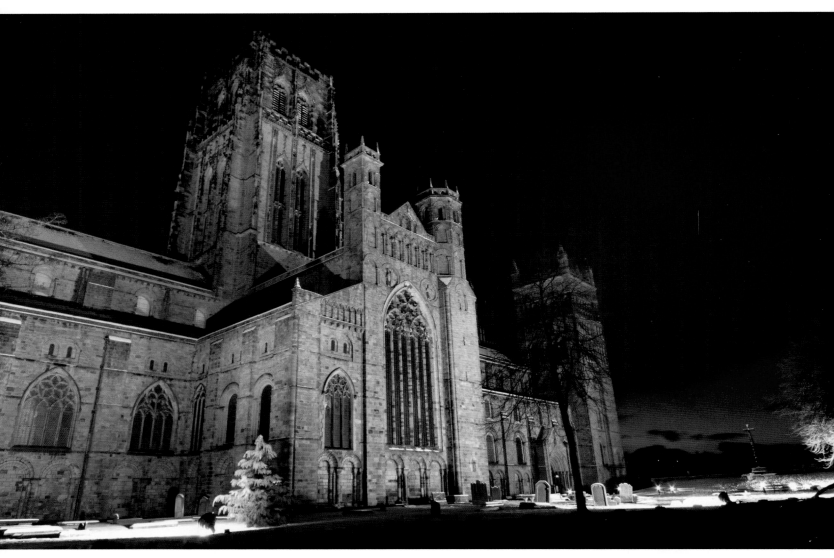

Durham Cathedral is one of the greatest churches ever built. It was started by William de St Calais (St Carileph) in 1093 and its main fabric was completed in 40 years.

The Cathedral dominates the skyline of the city from every direction – the rich autumn light
is particularly attractive in this view from South Street Mill landing stage.

The Cathedral towers reflected in the River Wear on an autumn afternoon.

The Cathedral high above the frozen River Wear, seen in icy splendour from Framwellgate Bridge.

The copy of the Sanctuary Knocker on the North Door of the Cathedral and...

...the original Sanctuary Knocker in the Cathedral Treasures. It was these two splendid examples that gave rise to the famous Blue Peter gaffe "What a beautiful pair of Knockers!" Grasping the Sanctuary Knocker would secure 37 days safety for a felon fleeing justice. Durham held the distinction of being able to grant *"Peculiar Sanctuary"* which meant that immunity could be granted for serious crimes such as High Treason. The only crime for which sanctuary could not be given was sacrilege. The system was abolished by King James I in 1624.

The Rose Window, high on the east wall of the Chapel of the Nine Altars, is 90 feet in circumference and depicts Christ in Majesty surrounded by the Twelve Apostles and the Crowned Elders.

St Cuthbert's Tomb. St Cuthbert died in 687AD and his body was brought to Durham in 995AD. In 1104 it was taken into the newly built Cathedral and placed in a magnificent new shrine which became a focus of pilgrimage during the Middle Ages when multitudes of people flocked to Durham to seek the Saint's blessing and healing powers.

The Transfiguration Window in memory of
Michael Ramsey, Archbishop of Canterbury from
1961–1974 who lived in Durham during three
periods of his life. He was a Professor of Divinity,
A Residentiary Canon of the Cathedral and later,
Bishop of Durham and lived in the City in
his retirement. The window was dedicated on
25 September 2010. Commissioned by the
Cathedral Chapter it was given by the Friends of
Durham Cathedral to mark their 75th anniversary
and made by Tom Denny in his Dorset studio.

The Chapel of the Nine Altars was designed by Richard of Farnham and built between 1242 and 1280. The large number of priests in the monastery had to say mass every day and so nine altars were provided – hence the name of the chapel. This arrangement also helped accommodate the great number of people visiting the Shrine of St Cuthbert.

Frosterley Marble is Durham's equivalent of Purbeck Marble. It is really a local limestone that is quarried near the village of Frosterley in Weardale. When sawn and polished the rock takes on a rich black or deep grey colour and the naturally present fossils show up as a contrasting white random pattern. This makes the unique Frosterley Marble a most attractive but functional decorative building material.

The Miners' Memorial stands near the south door that leads
into the cloisters. Coal mining was once the major industry
in County Durham and the miners have always had a close
association with the Cathedral. Every year, on the first weekend
in July, a moving service is held as part of the Miners' Gala.

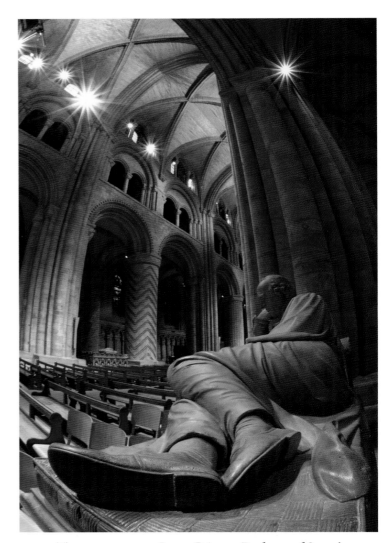

The monument to James Britton, Professor of Sacred
Theology, at one time the Headmaster of Durham School.
The pupils of Durham School have a great affinity with the
Cathedral – they traditionally call it 'The Abbey'.

The St Cuthbert Window above the door at the north-west end of the nave was given by the Friends of Durham Cathedral and installed in 1945.
It suffered damage during a gale on Friday 13 1984 and was subsequently repaired. This window, together with another, similar, in the south-west end of the nave was designed by Hugh Easton.

The Millennium Window was dedicated in 1997 in celebration of the 1000th anniversary – in AD995 – of the arrival of St Cuthbert's body in Durham. It was designed by Joseph Nuttgens of High Wycombe and the glass was supplied by the local firm of Hartley Woods of Sunderland. The window depicts significant key events and developments in the county over the last 1000 years.

The Daily Bread Window was the gift of the staff of Marks & Spencer in Durham to commemorate the firm's centenary year. It is a modern design that represents the Last Supper, by Mark Angus of Bath. The hand-blown antique glass was supplied by Hartley Woods of Sunderland.

The absolute quintessence of the magnificent stonework of Durham Cathedral can be seen in the nave pillars. They are alternatively decorated cylindrical piers and composite cluster piers.

The bones of the Venerable Bede were brought to Durham in 1022 and were placed in a magnificent shrine in 1370. However this was destroyed by King Henry's men at the Reformation in 1540 and his bones were buried in their present place. Bede died in 735AD. He is famous as a scholar and historian and wrote the first History of England and documented the Life of St Cuthbert, an account that is particularly valuable since Bede's life started just when Cuthbert's life ended and he was able to interview many of Cuthbert's contemporaries during his work. He is popularly known as "The Father of English History".

The light and delicate architecture of the Chapel is in striking contrast to the earlier, more massive part of the building. Although the difficulties of creating high vaults to carry the huge stone roof had been overcome in the main part of the Cathedral, the Galilee was given a low timber roof which allows light into the western end of the nave and aisles through the large west window. The Galilee Chapel had three functions – as a place of worship for women, who weren't allowed into the main part of the Cathedral – as a processional space – and as an ecclesiastical court.

In the wall alcoves of the modern altar in the Galilee Chapel are two life-size wall paintings, dating from the time of the Galilee's construction in the twelfth century. Some historians believe these to be of St Cuthbert *(above left)* and St Oswald *(above centre)*. Sadly the Oswald painting is incomplete but an impression *(above right)* skilfully reconstructed by artist Sophy Nixon shows how it may have looked in its original form.

Above the arcading in the Galilee Chapel this series of wall paintings dates from the thirteenth or fourteenth centuries and depicts the crucifixion of Christ and the apostles as martyrs, dying for their faith.

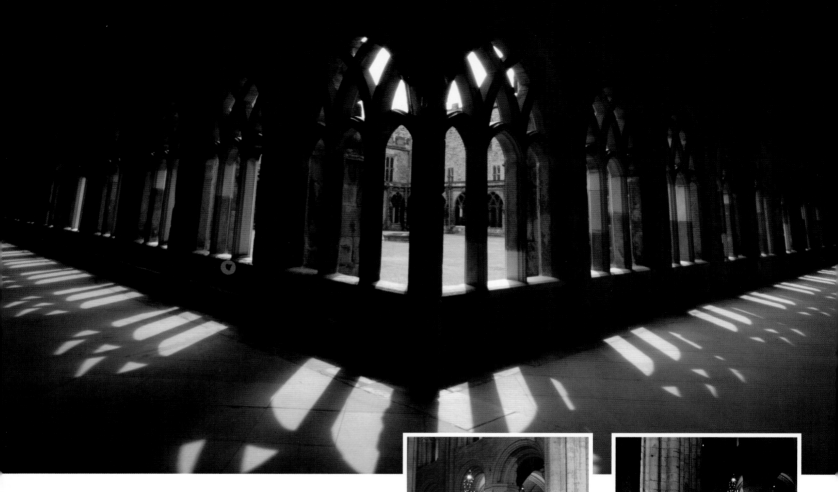

The cloister was the centre of daily life for a monk. The cloister at Durham was built on the instructions of Bishops Langley and Skirlaw. It was started in 1368 under Langley but the work dragged on slowly up to the time of Bishop Skirlaw and was not finally finished until 1498. Originally the windows would have been glazed – one series is said to have told the story of St Cuthbert in its stained glass.

Right: In spite of its architectural vastness there is still an intimate warmth and comfort in Durham Cathedral at Christmas time.

Dun Cow Lane takes its name from the panel on the north-west turret of the Chapel of the Nine Altars, but was originally called Lyegate or Lykegate because this would have been the road along which the bodies were brought for burial.

The eastern end of the Cathedral, with its large buttresses and Rose Window seen from Dun Cow Lane.

The Durham Light Infantry Memorial Gardens commemorate Durham's own regiment. The DLI was formed in 1758 but its individual identity disappeared in 1968 when it merged with three other regiments to become known simply as 'The Light Infantry'. The 'Faithfuls', as they were known, had seen action in every theatre of war from the West Indies to the swamps and jungles of Borneo.

The Dark Entry.

A long ramp leads up to the College Buildings from Prebends' Bridge. It was constructed so that any attacking force had its right side exposed, unprotected by shields held on the left arm. The ramp leads into the Dark Entry, an eerie tunnel that leads into the College and was once the site of the entrance to the Monastery Guest House.

The Keep, Durham Castle. Durham Castle was built in 1072 by William I and was the main seat or Palace of the Bishops of Durham until 1837, when it became the home of University College.

The Gatehouse, Durham Castle. This magnificent addition to the castle was the work of Bishop Hugh le Puiset (Pudsey) in the second half of the twelfth century, although it was later altered by Bishop Cuthbert Tunstall in the mid 1500s and improved yet again by Bishop Shute Barrington when he held office in the late 1700s and early 1800s.

The coats of arms of four important men are colourfully picked out on a cartouche on the wall above 'Cosin's Porch', as this entrance to the Great Hall of Durham Castle is known. They belong to Bishop John Cosin, Bishop Thomas Hatfield, Robert Grey, who was a canon during Cosin's term of office, and William Westley who was archdeacon of Durham and Bishop Hatfield's chancellor. Below this is the coat of arms of Prince Bishop, John Cosin.

The Great Hall was probably built by Bishop Bek in about 1300. It was enlarged by Bishop Hatfield in 1350 and then reduced to its original size by Bishop Fox who added the Minstrels' Gallery. Many important people have dined in this hall including Her Majesty Queen Elizabeth II, and on one occasion Sir Walter Scott and the Duke of Wellington dined together with Bishop William van Mildert on 3 October 1827.

The Norman Chapel in Durham Castle is built in a style that is typical of the years between 1070 and 1080, and is regarded as the most important example in the county of early Norman architecture. It has a wonderful atmosphere and the capitals of its columns, decorated in an almost barbaric style of leaves, faces and beasts, add greatly to its atmosphere.

The Exchequer was built by Bishop Neville about 1450 and housed the courts of Halmote, Pleas and Chancery as well as other various Palatinate courts. The bull's head high on the wall above the doorway represents the crest of the Nevilles. This was one of the first buildings on the Palace Green taken over by the university.

Bishop Cosin's Library dates from 1669 and was used by the Diocesan Clergy. When the university was founded in 1833 a gallery was added, together with an extra front door to be used by the students.

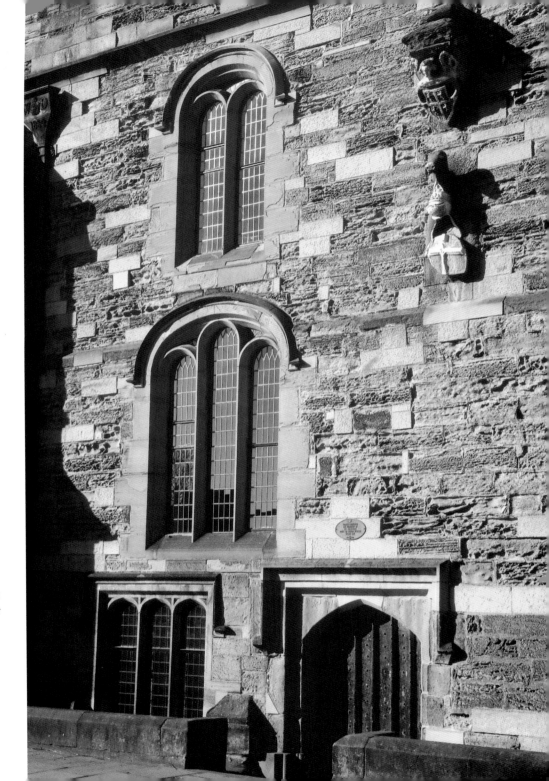

Graduation at the university takes place in June in a location that is possibly the best in the world.
The students are robed in the Great Hall of the Castle and process to the
Cathedral where the ceremony takes place.

Durham University Music School is regarded as one of the leading centres for the study of music in Britain. A talented international staff of musicologists, composers and performers – leading figures in their fields – offer expertise in a notably wide range of musical areas, and the department attracts students from all over the world to work in an intellectually stimulating environment.

Owengate. The origin of this street name is unknown but it has one of the oldest houses in the city, a timber-framed building dating from the sixteenth century. The house is most attractive with typical oversailing upper storeys; however the top storey is not original. The street leads up to the Palace Green to reveal to visitors their first breathtaking view of the Cathedral.

Bow Lane leads down to the river and was once called 'Kingsgate'. It was so named because when William the Conqueror was in Durham he insisted on seeing for himself whether the body of St Cuthbert was really uncorrupted. When the king was about to enter the Cathedral he was suddenly seized by a 'great panic and excessive heat' – he leapt on his horse and galloped down Kingsgate with great speed and, it is said, did not stop until he had crossed the Tees safely into Yorkshire.

Cathedral and Kingsgate Bridge – the bridge was an unusual feat of engineering. It was built in two halves, each parallel to their respective river bank and on completion they were swung out to meet perfectly in the middle of the river.

Dunelm House, the headquarters of the Students' Union, framed by Kingsgate
Bridge, its outline softened by the trees of the River Banks.

St Oswald's Church dates from the twelfth century but is said to stand on the site of an earlier Saxon Church. It was rebuilt in 1834 by the noted architect Ignatius Bonomi. The dedication is to St Oswald who defeated the pagan hoards of Cadwallon at the Battle of Heavenfield in 634AD and thus re-established a foothold for Christianity in Northumbria.

The Bailey was once part of the inner defences of the city – this attractive town house is now part of St John's College. Fortunately its tall buildings and quiet cobbled streets have changed little over the years.

A view of the Bailey showing the old "Stink Pipe", a clever invention to utilise sewer gas to provide street lighting, thus avoiding a build-up of pressure in the sewers and avoiding the unpleasant consequences of an explosion. This is allegedly the origin of the popular song *"My Grandmother's Fatha* (sic) *Was a Stink Pipe Lighter"*, often heard in the folk and country clubs of Durham.

The Bailey is one of the finest streets in the city and is not only an interesting mix of buildings, several people of note have lived here. Ignatius Bonomi the celebrated architect lived at number 5. John Gully, who served time in debtor's prison but later rose to fame as a bare-knuckle prize fighter and went on to be a colliery owner and a Member of Parliament, also lived in this street. Other residents, included the Earls of Strathmore, ancestors of the present Royal Family, and the Liddell family, wealthy coal owners, one of whose daughters was Alice Liddell who, it is said, inspired *Alice in Wonderland*.

Alms Houses, Assembly rooms and Divinity Building comprise an interesting range of architecture on the Palace Green.
The Alms Houses were originally associated with Bishop Langley but were rebuilt by Bishop John Cosin for
eight poor men and women. There was a school at each end – one for grammar and one for song.

The College is the name given to the Cathedral Garth. Apart from the Choristers School and administration buildings it also is the site of the homes of many of the key people of the Cathedral.

'Order and Chaos', a sculpture representing the Bishop's Throne, or Cathedra, was created
by Colin Wilbourne while he was Artist in Residence at Durham Cathedral.

One of the many boathouses that can be found along the River Banks in the City - this one is at the eastern end of the weir between the Fulling Mill and South Street Mill, looking towards Framwellgate Bridge.

South Street Mill, also known as The Priors Cornmill, would have served all the tenants of the priory lands in the Barony of Elvet. It is however of uncertain date and was not recorded in the Boldon Book of 1185 but there is evidence to suggest it existed and was indeed working in the late fourteenth century.

Even in winter the network of paths around the River Banks provide beautiful walking.

The Old Fulling Mill is now the Museum of Archaeology. It dates from the start of the fifteenth century and was part of the newly-established weaving trade which was then growing in the city.

Grey Towers of Durham
Yet well I love thy mixed and massive piles;
Half Church of God half castle 'gainst the Scot
And long to roam these venerable aisles
With records stored of deeds long since forgot.

The famous words of Sir Walter Scott, anciently engraved on Prebends' Bridge, were composed, we are told, when he was dining with Prince Bishop William van Mildert in Durham Castle. Some say he dashed it off on a serviette while he was waiting for his pudding!

Prebends' Bridge was built in 1777 at the expense of the Prebends or Canons of the Cathedral. It was designed by George Nicholson and replaced the earlier one of 1574 which was washed away in the Great Flood of 1771. Prior to 1574 a ferry operated here.

Shipperdson's Cottage is sometimes mistakenly called the Little Counts House. Count Josef Boruwlaski's house was nearby but was demolished after his death. This cottage was built in the 1820s as a garden retreat for Mr Shipperdson who lived in the South Bailey at the top of the steep wooded hillside.

The Camera Obscura is an unusual piece of public sculpture constructed from the stones of one of the badly eroded eastern spires of the Chapel of the Nine Altars of the Cathedral. When it was decided to replace the spires, stonework from one was reconstructed on the western side of Prebends' Bridge. The central tower of the Cathedral can be seen through the carefully sited aperture in the work.

The Banksman's Cottage has also been known as Prebends Cottage and Betsy's Cottage. It was probably built at the same time as Prebends' Bridge. In the late 1700s it served as a dwelling for the banksman employed by the Dean and Chapter to manage the river banks and keep the footpaths free from obstruction.

The River Banks. An excellent network of footpaths is found around the peninsula on both sides of the river and connected by several bridges, both ancient and modern, providing a wonderful variety of invigorating or relaxing walking at any time of year.

The *Prince Bishop* River Cruiser not only provides an opportunity to see Durham
from its river aspect but also offers the chance to enjoy barbecue cruises in
the summer and Christmas parties during the festive season.

The site of the remains of the Chapel of St Andrew on the south-east corner of Elvet Bridge. Chapels on bridges were common in medieval times because bridge building and repairing were considered to be religious duties. There was also a similar chapel, dedicated to St James, built on the north-west corner of the bridge, but no trace of this now remains.

Boat Hire in the City near Elvet Bridge allows the opportunity to admire Durham's sylvan River Banks – either downstream to enjoy impressive close-up views of the Cathedral, or upstream through more rural scenery to take in a more distant aspect.

Elvet Bridge and Durham Cathedral. The Cathedral dominates the city skyline from every view. Elvet Bridge was built by Bishop Pudsey in 1160 and repaired by Bishop Fox in 1495. Three arches were washed away in the Great Flood of 1771, which destroyed or badly damaged most of the bridges in north-east England. The bridge was doubled in width in the early 1800s but the early work can still be seen between the ribs under the southern end. In addition to the two chapels at either end of the bridge there would have also been a toll booth to take advantage of the opportunity to collect revenue from travellers making their way into the city.

Morris Dancers on Elvet Bridge. A dancing competition that attracts
entrants from all over the North is part of the July Summer Festival.

The floodlit Cathedral is an unforgettable sight when approaching the city from Leazes Road and the
A1 motorway. The floodlighting of the Cathedral was started in the mid sixties by Norman Richardson,
businessman, Alderman, former Mayor and honorary Freeman of the City.

Durham from Pelaw Wood . This wood was presented to the City of Durham by Lord Londonderry in the 1930s. Unfortunately the pathways and bank sides were eroding into the river and so a strong retaining wall was built to solve the problem.

To the north of the City a well managed network of footpaths offer excellent opportunities for walking – many are described in the author's *A Boot Up Durham City*, also available from Halsgrove.

The Prince Bishops Shopping Centre was opened on 18 December 1998 by the then MP for Durham, Gerry Steinberg. It was constructed to give what is, in effect, two extra streets to the city in keeping with its existing design. The outside of the development is a representation of the architect's interpretation of how the ancient city walls would have appeared. However the green tiles on the face of the eastern stairwell of the car park have met with a fair amount of disapproval.

Saddler Street is one of the oldest streets in Durham and was once the site of a mustard factory. This is where Mrs Clements is said to have first ground mustard seeds to make Durham Mustard in 1720. In its day it was famous throughout the land and it is said that King George II was one of its keenest users.

The Kemble Gallery and the Shakespeare Inn have more in common than first it would seem – they both serve as a reminder that Durham's main theatre was once in this area. The illustrious Stephen Kemble was once the manager and it was his daughter Fanny who achieved fame and fortune on the London stage with her great beauty, her singing and her popular performances.

Elvet Bridge, looking towards Saddler Street. 'Outside tables' at coffee shops and restaurants are becoming more widespread as the medieval city embraces European 'café-culture'.

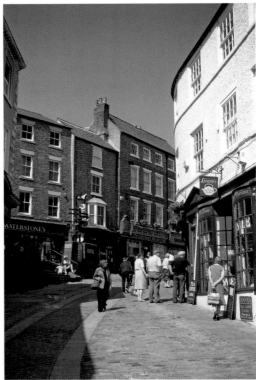

Looking towards Fleshergate from Elvet Bridge. Fleshergate was the butchers' area. There are accounts from the early nineteenth century of butchers slaughtering animals in front of their shops and blood and piles of offal being left in the street. Fortunately this was all brought to an end with the health reforms of the nineteenth century.

The entrance to the Indoor Market. Trade has been going on here since 1851
and there are over 60 stalls to supply the needs of keen shoppers.

Neptune's statue was restored to the Market Place in May 1991. It was originally given to the City by George Bowes, MP of Gibside and Streatlam, as a reminder of the scheme that was put forward to link Durham to the sea by dredging the River Wear that would have seen ocean-going boats moored near to the Market Place. However the plan did not come to fruition and Neptune was eventually placed on top of Durham's new 'pant' (a kind of public fountain) in 1902. Thomas Hutchinson, the noted Durham historian, was very taken with the supply and proclaimed that 'It is a fluent fountain of most excellent water'. When the pant was demolished the statue was removed to Wharton Park but after a few years, in spite being struck by lightning on one occasion, it was returned to the Market Place.

The Londonderry Statue. The statue of Charles William Vane Stewart the 3rd Marquess of Londonderry is arguably one of the finest equestrian statues in the world. It was sculpted by Rafaelle Monti of Milan and is constructed with quarter-inch copper plate on plaster, the first time this process had been used on such a grand scale. Legend has it that when it was finished Monti declared it to be perfect and offered a substantial financial reward to anyone who could find fault. A blind beggar took up the challenge and felt the inside of the horse's mouth with his staff and declared that the horse had no tongue. Monti was devastated. He was so distraught that he committed suicide – however he must have done this very slowly because he didn't actually die until 20 years after the alleged incident, and, of course, the horse does have a tongue.

The Durham City Summer Festival takes place on the first week in July – it dates back to the old medieval fairs that took place on saints' days – particularly the two festivals of St Cuthbert that were held in March and September. The streets are filled with music and dancers and, together with a wide variety of stalls and crafts on display, this make an event that attracts many visitors.

Durham City's controversial re-vamped market place – part of the 'Durham City Vision', £5.25m 'Heart of the City' project which has fuelled much heated debate and generated a petition against signed by almost 6000 people.

The new lighting and seating in the revamped Market Place, creating more space. The cleverly designed seating allows short people to sit at one end and taller people at the other.

Looking into the Market Place from what was once Fleshergate. The Town Hall and Guildhall were originally built in 1356 but were rebuilt with several improvements by Bishop Cuthbert Tunstall in the mid 1500s. The Guildhall was restored by Bishop Cosin in 1665 and further extensive building was done between 1752 and 1754. The Arms of eleven of the City Freemen's Guilds can be seen on the walls – these men played an important part in civic life between fourteenth and sixteenth centuries. A new Town Hall, financed by public subscription, was opened in 1851. It was grandly designed on the lines of Westminster Hall. On each side of the Great Fireplace are panels displaying the names of the honorary Freemen of the City. The Indoor Market, just to the left, has been going since 1851 and there are over 60 stalls to supply the needs of the keen shoppers.

Framwellgate Bridge was built across the river in 1126 by Bishop Ralph Flambard and carried one of the main roadways into the city. In the 1400s it was quite badly damaged by floods and was rebuilt to greater strength by Bishop Langley. A gate-house once stood at the eastern end of the bridge but it was removed in 1760 to ease the flow of traffic. Legend has it that a live toad, presumed to have been walled in many years before, was discovered by masons when further work was being carried out on the bridge in the mid nineteenth century.

The Town Hall and Guildhall were originally built in 1356 but were rebuilt with several improvements by Bishop Cuthbert Tunstall in the mid 1500s.

The west window of the Town Hall was designed by a local artist; the side lights represent the four Bishops of Durham who granted charters to the City – Pudsey, Pilkington, Matthew and Crewe. The upper lights represent the Corpus Christi procession of the guilds to the Cathedral and the lower lights portray Edward III on his return from an expedition against the Scots and thanking the citizens of Durham for rescuing his baggage train which was left unguarded during his absence.

Life-size statue of The Little Count and a display of clothes and possessions in the Town Hall. Count Josef Boruwlaski was born in Poland in 1739 but spent the last fifteen years of his remarkably long life in Durham, dying at the age of 79. He was an intellectual and an accomplished musician and freely associated with royalty and nobility. And yet he was an unfortunate man who sometimes felt humiliated, because he was a dwarf. He was only 3 feet 3 inches in height although he was perfectly proportioned. He was great friends with Stephen Kemble, the noted Shakespearean actor – they must have made an incongruous site walking the river banks together – Kemble was well over 6 feet tall and at one time weighed almost 22 stones. Count Josef Boruwlaski is buried in Durham Cathedral just below the RAF memorial window under a simple slab marked 'JB'.

Durham Miners' Gala is more popularly known as 'Durham Big Meeting'. Today the event is only a shadow of its former self – there is now no coal mining in the county – but for years on the third Saturday in July it was the focal point for every miner and his family. At its height it was the biggest meeting of the working classes anywhere in the country and up to the mid twentieth century it attracted crowds of over a hundred thousand people.

The Millennium Square was officially opened on the 8 June 2002 by Her Majesty the Queen as part of the Golden Jubilee Celebrations. The Square houses the Citizens' Advice Bureau, Clayport Library and the famous Gala Theatre, amid a wide selection of cafés, bars and restaurants.

Leazes road was constructed in 1967 to help ease the serious traffic congestion in the middle of the City.

Durham's 100 feet high Viaduct carries the main London to Edinburgh railway line high above the city. It was built in 1857 by North East Railways engineer Mr T E Harrison. Because the ground it crossed was extremely soft, oak piles had to be driven into the earth to support the eleven arches of this remarkable piece of Victorian engineering.

Gilesgate Bank was once one of the main roads in and out of the city.

The church of St Mary-le-Bow takes its name from the arch that spanned Bow Lane here and formed, together with the old church tower, part of the fortifications that formed an inner defence if the Bow Lane Gate was breached. The church tower collapsed in 1637 and destroyed the arch and much of the nave; consequently the church was rebuilt in early 1700. It now houses the Durham Heritage Centre.

Durham Cathedral from the South Street Mill landing-stage in winter. The almost
frozen River Wear compliments this icy but tranquil scene.

St Margaret's Church. In AD306 Margaret was the daughter of a heathen priest in Antioch who became a Christian when she was disowned by her father. The local governor was particularly taken with her and wanted to marry her, or indeed buy her if she was a slave. Margaret said she was free but was a slave of Jesus Christ. She suffered for her faith – she was imprisoned, tortured and eventually decapitated.

St Margaret's is the burial place of Sir John Duck – Durham's equivalent of Dick Whittington. He arrived in Durham penniless and wanted to be a butcher, but was not allowed to join the Guild. Eventually John Heslop gave him a job against their wishes. He married the boss's daughter but the Guild imposed a heavy fine on Heslop and he was left with no alternative but to dismiss Duck. To avoid creating any more difficulties for his father-in-law he made plans to leave the city. John Duck was on the banks of the river, making his way towards Framwellgate Bridge when a raven dropped a gold coin at his feet. He met a farmer on the bridge having trouble with two cows he was driving to market – Duck used the coin to buy these beasts, drove them to the market himself, and made a good profit. He went on to be a very successful cattle dealer and eventually began to trade as a butcher. His businesses made a large amount of money and he became a highly respected citizen. In 1680 he was made Mayor of Durham and given the freedom of the Butchers' Company. He used some of his money to buy an estate at Haswell and became the owner of several coal mines. In 1668 he founded a hospital at Lumley, was knighted by Charles II and he and his wife moved into their house at the top of Silver Street. Sir John Duck died in 1691, aged 59 – his wife, Anne, died in 1695. They are buried side-by-side in the church.

South Street is one of Durham's most sought after addresses; from here there are magnificent views of the Castle and the western aspect of the Cathedral. It has been suggested that the street dates back to Roman times. Indeed, until a couple of hundred years ago it was one of the main routes out of the city. The road surface still has its cobbles or sets, which would have been a great help to horses in keeping a strong foothold on the steep hill.

Pimlico was once the artists' area of Durham. Stephen Kemble, the actor and theatre manager and great friend of Count Josef Boruwlaski lived here at 'The Grove' in the early nineteenth century.

The Silver Link Bridge on the edge of
Pelaw Wood was built across Pelaw Beck to
commemorate the Silver Jubilee of George V.
Prior to this a precarious steep descent,
followed by a very stiff climb, was the only
way to negotiate this deep ravine.

The Vane Tempest Hall in Gilesgate is the only surviving example of a Militia Barracks in County Durham. The Durham Militia was formed in 1759; officers were chosen from the local gentry and the rank-and-file men were selected by ballot. In 1893 the building was bought by Lord Londonderry to use as the headquarters of the Second Durham Artillery Volunteers. Today the building is used as a busy community centre but it is reputed to haunted by the ghost of a soldier who was executed in the courtyard for mutiny.

St Giles Church was founded by Bishop Flambard and dedicated by him on 11 June 1112. A hospital was originally associated with the church but because of the soft nature of the ground and consequent problems with the fabric of the building it was rebuilt on another site at a later date. There is an effigy of John Heath of Kepier in the church – he was a friend of Bernard Gilpin and together they founded the Kepier School in Houghton-le-Spring. During the time St Godric lived in Durham he was a member of the congregation of St Giles and eventually became a doorman and a bell-ringer.

Gilesgate, or Gillygate as it was known, still has an old-style village green. One area is even called the Duck Pond, although this has long since dried up. It was once part of one of the main ancient roadways into the city.

The Chapel of St Mary Magdalene was once the chapel of a small hospital formed in the early eleventh century. In 1391 an indulgence was granted by Bishop Walter Skirlaw to all those who gave it support. After the Dissolution in 1546 the chapel was still used as a place of worship and this continued right up to the end of the seventeenth century when it fell into disuse after the building had become unsafe.

Kepier Hospital. It was this building, down by the river at Kepier, that replaced the original at St Giles in about 1180. It housed poor and feeble old men who were unable to work. However they were expected to attend church services for the good of their souls since little could be done for their physical well-being except the provision of food, a comfortable place to rest and cleanliness. Sadly most were only in care a few years before they died.

An observation window can be seen high in a gable end at the junction of Gilesgate and Claypath, strategically placed to look out for invaders from the coast who would approach from the east.

Tinklers' Lane is the place where tinkers repaired or sold pots and pans because they were banned from the city streets.

The wall mural on the gable end of the houses on Gilesgate Bank was
painted to commemorate the 900th anniversary of the Cathedral.

Old Durham. Some historians believe that Old Durham was settled as far back as the Iron Age; the name, however, was not used until 1268 when the settlement belonged to the Parish of St Nicholas. By 1443 it came into the possession of Kepier Hospital. In 1578 it passed into the ownership of John Heath who dissolved the hospital at Kepier. It then passed through an heiress of the Heaths to the Tempests and it was they who built the Manor House and the pleasant walled garden.

Old Durham gardens were a popular weekend attraction in the 1920s. The walled garden and the gazebo were all that was left of the Tempest's Manor House but there was dancing here, a putting green, a running track, tennis courts and a tea garden. The Pineapple Inn was attached to the gardens but by 1926 the landlord had fallen foul of the licensing laws and was only able to sell soft drinks.

Pelaw Wood was presented to the City of Durham by Lord Londonderry in the 1930s. The pathways and bank sides were eroding into the Wear and so a strong retaining wall was constructed to prevent further problems.

Maiden Castle footbridge was designed by the award winning architects Ove Arup in 1972; it links the University sports hall and the new Nobby Stiles Boathouse with the rugby and football pitches across the river.

Drummer Boy's Hole. In the late 1700s the ford across the river at the eastern end of Pelaw Wood was a dangerous place to cross and great care had to be taken. A story from that time tells of how on one winter's evening, just as darkness fell, a young Drummer Boy with the Durham Militia missed his footing crossing the ford and stumbled into a hole and drowned in the icy water, in spite of frantic attempts at rescue by his colleagues. They say on a winter's night the sound of a drum can be faintly heard as the ghost of the young Drummer Boy tries to cross the ford again.

Maiden Castle is crowned by an Iron Age fort standing some hundred feet above the surrounding
countryside. Substantial remains are clearly visible at the western end of the summit.
There is a ditch almost thirty feet wide which would, presumably, have been crossed
by a drawbridge and a nine feet high encircling wall in support, completing the defences.

The country walks through Houghall wood are a delight – especially in spring when the first flowers are in bloom. Industrial remains softened by nature form the basis for an interesting Discovery Trail.

The Old Racecourse seen from the bandstand. The fist mention of a racecourse in Durham was in the press in 1773 although the first mention of horse-racing dates back to 1665. Race meetings were held twice a year in April and July until 1887 when they clashed with the Miners' Big Meeting. In 1888 the Race Committee reluctantly surrendered their lease to the University and the course was closed – but by then some officials in the city thought that the races had 'degenerated into a very disreputable affair'. A new racecourse was built at Shincliffe.

The Durham Cow is a public sculpture by Andrew Burton. A cow features in the legend of the discovery of Dunholm in the search to find a final resting place for the body of St Cuthbert. However we are led to believe that this was a dun-coloured Durham Shorthorn.

The Bandstand sited on the riverside walk opposite Pelaw Wood. This replaced the nearby original in which a band played most weekends.

Durham Regatta is one of the oldest in the country. It is held at the beginning of June when local teams, together with others from all over the country, compete for honours.

Baths Bridge links Elvet with Claypath and Gilesgate. A succession of footbridges has crossed the river at this point. The first one was built in 1855, at the same time as the swimming baths; this was replaced by a substantial iron girder bridge in 1898, and finally the present concrete arch, a copy of the original, was opened in 1962.

Durham from Pelaw Wood.   The riverside footpath is an easy walk to the nearby village of Shincliffe..

A view of the Castle and Cathedral from the railway station. This is part of what was once referred to as Ruskin's View – the said John Ruskin seemed to be very keen on various "views" and had many favourites of these in numerous parts of the country.

Framwellgate Bridge was built across the river in 1126 by Bishop Ralph Flambard and carried one of the main roadways into the city. In the 1400s it was quite badly damaged by floods and was rebuilt to greater strength by Bishop Langley. A gatehouse once stood at the eastern end of the bridge but it was removed in 1760 to ease the flow of traffic. Legend has it that it was here that the live toad, referred to earlier, was discovered by masons when further work was being carried out on the bridge in the mid nineteenth century.

The Pennyferry Bridge was built by the City Council as part of the Millennium celebrations. Its name, decided in a competition, recalls that a ferry used to operate near this spot in medieval times.

Either rowing for pleasure, just messing about in boats or intense
practice for one of the several regattas, the river Wear attracts
rowers in all seasons.

Autumn reflections in the Wear in Kepier Wood. A pleasant riverside woodland walk within easy access from Claypath and Gilesgate, its sylvan tranquillity belies the fact that it was once a scene of busy industry – two mines and a stone quarry have worked here in the past. Tradition has it that some of the stone used in the building of Durham Cathedral was quarried here. This ancient woodland once extended much nearer the city centre but extensive tree-felling in the late nineteenth century caused a public outcry and left, according to the *Durham County Advertiser* "an area of complete devastation".

Some historians believe that Crook Hall manor house dates from 1286, although the house probably originates from sometime in the fourteenth century, built by Peter de Croke, hence the name, Crook Hall. It was his daughter, Joan de Croke who married John de Copeland the English knight who had his front teeth knocked out capturing King David of Scotland after the Battle of Neville's Cross.

Near the old Shakespeare Inn a secluded vennel, Moatside Lane, connects Saddler Street with Silver Street, following the line of the old Castle Moat – hence its name; although some historians argue that it derives from *Motte-Side*, taking its name from the fact that the castle is built on a *motte* , or artificial mound. Whatever the truth it's a pleasurably sinister short cut.

Trevelyan College was opened in 1967 and is an innovative design of simple interlocking
hexagonal buildings for which it won a Civic Trust Award. The College takes its name from
the famous historian, G. M. Trevelyan, a former Chancellor of the University.

St Aidan's College, situated high on Windmill Hill, was designed
by noted architect Sir Basil Spence and opened in 1964.

St Mary's College, seen from the central tower of the Cathedral, dates from 1952
and exclusively catered for women students until quite recently.

The Oriental Museum in Durham is the only one of its kind in Great Britain. Its collections are wide ranging and cover subjects ranging from ancient Egypt, India and the Islamic World to the Far Eastern cultures of China and Japan.
The museum was established in 1950 and opened to the public in 1960. It is part of Durham University and its excellent collections not only provide pleasure for visitors but are also available to academics for research and learning.

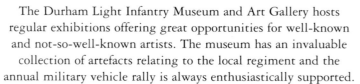

The Durham Light Infantry Museum and Art Gallery hosts regular exhibitions offering great opportunities for well-known and not-so-well-known artists. The museum has an invaluable collection of artefacts relating to the local regiment and the annual military vehicle rally is always enthusiastically supported.

Extensive tree felling on the river banks a few years ago revealed a remarkable "new view" of the Cathedral.

The Battle of Neville's Cross sculpture in
The Durham Johnston School Grounds.

The Battle of Neville's Cross was fought on
17 October 1346 between the Scots under
King David II and the English led by Sir
Ralph Neville, Henry Percy and the
Archbishop of York. It is regarded as one
of the most important Border battles of its
time. After a short, bloody fight the Scots
were defeated and their king captured. As
a reward for the victory Ralph Neville was
granted the honour of being the first
layman to be allowed burial in Durham
Cathedral. Local legend has it that if you
walk three times round the cross and then
put your ear to the ground you will hear
the sound of the clash of arms.

Durham Cathedral and reflection from South Street Mill landing stage. An iconic view of what is "probably the most beautiful religious building in the world", a view quite rightly expressed by the readers of *The London Evening Standard*, a few years ago.

Sherburn Hospital Gatehouse. In the late 1100s Bishop Hugh Pudsey, one of the most powerful of the Prince Bishops, built a hospital for 65 monks and nuns suffering from leprosy. Later when the disease had stopped being regarded as such a threat patients suffering from other complaints were allowed treatment. By the sixteenth century the building had badly deteriorated and much rebuilding and improvement was carried out in Georgian and Victorian times. Today the building is a retirement and care home.

Pittington is an old mining village and its beautiful twelfth century Church of St Laurence is situated at the end of an old lane surrounded by a wooded burial ground. It was partly rebuilt in 1847 by Ignatius Bonomi. However some of the most exciting architecture in the county incorporated into its fabric is still to be seen. The north arcade was built by Bishop Pudsey and the designs of the columns clearly relate to those in Durham Cathedral. The chief treasure of the church must be the pair of adjacent twelfth-century wall paintings depicting the consecration of St Cuthbert and an interpretation of his vision at the table of the Abbess Alfled.

A midsummer agricultural landscape looking from the village of Sherburn across the fields to Pittington.

Highgate from St Godric's Church. A new development on the western side of the city in the Milburngate and Framwellgate area, the modern houses are tastefully designed and echo the architecture that once stood here and are beautifully blended to harmonise with the traditional look of the city.

Combine harvesting on Sherburn Farm – at this busy period work can go on late into the evening.
It is hard to believe that agriculture is a major industry within the city boundaries.

Ludworth Tower is one of Durham's few Pele Towers. Permission to fortify his manor house was given to Roger Holden by Bishop Langley in 1422. The tunnel-vaulted basement can still be seen together with the remains of a three-storeyed wall, a fireplace and a spiral staircase. It stands as a silent monument to those more unsettled times of border raiding.

St. Godric's Church is beautifully situated overlooking Durham City Centre. It was built in 1864 and in 1909 it was extended and the tower was added. In 1985 it was badly damaged by fire, but after extensive restoration it was reopened. Its dedication is to Saint Godric of Finchale a hermit, merchant and popular medieval saint. He was born in Walpole in Norfolk and died on the site of the present day Finchale Priory, just a few miles from his church, along the River Wear.

William Lloyd Wharton gave use of Windy Hill to the City in July 1858 making Wharton Park one of the earliest public parks in the region, although he retained ownership of the land. Apparently his intentions were to provide a public park for the city and to safeguard that area from development. The *Durham Advertiser* commented 'The genius of the age shows itself in nothing more gratifying than the various attempts which are now making to provide wholesome places of exercise and recreation for the great bulk of the working classes'. The first Miners' Gala was held here in 1871.

Finchale Priory is perhaps Durham's most
notable monastic ruin. It was founded in
1100 by St Godric who was so influenced by
the cult of St Cuthbert that he gave up his
life as a pedlar, a sailor and (some even
venture) a pirate, to pursue a life of penance
as a hermit in 'this snake-infested spot' by the
River Wear. We are told he wore nothing but
sackcloth – spent nearly all night up to his
neck in cold water praying, and that he would
only eat his food when it was rotten and
would bake ashes from the fire into his bread.
It didn't seem to do him much harm because
he died at Finchale in 1170 at 105 years of
age. In 1196 Finchale became a priory for
nine monks of Durham – four would come
on a three-week rota to join the Prior of
Finchale and his four resident monks – this is
why it is often referred to as a 'holiday home'
for the monks of Durham. An unsettling
legend tells of a long, dark tunnel linking
Finchale with Durham Cathedral that has
been sealed up because it is so full of
horrors that no man can stand the journey
through its dank depths.

Finchale Priory undercroft.

The Kingfisher Bridge carries the riverside cycle path and walkway over Old Durham Beck.
One of Durham's newest bridges it was opened on the 18 December 2007 at a cost of £125,000.

Beau Repaire stands just across the River Browney from the former mining village of Bearpark. The name is translated as 'beautiful retreat' and it was an important country residence for the Priors of Durham. The original manor house was built by Prior Bartram of Middleton in 1258 and the licence to enclose the surrounding lands and create a park was granted in 1267. By the early fourteenth century the cesspit had been replaced by a flush toilet which was connected to the dormitory and chapel. The manor house suffered extensive and repeated destruction at the hands of the Scots in their regular raids in the mid 1600s although the small section they left standing was still at roof height in 1787. But all that can be seen today are low walls and earthworks.

Aldin Grange Bridge is one of Durham's oldest bridges but it has now been bypassed by the late-nineteenth century bridge alongside. Its claim to fame is in the local story that tells of how King David of Scotland hid underneath it after his defeat at the Battle of Neville's Cross, only to be discovered by his reflection in the River Browney. John de Copeland was the English knight who captured him, although the king did not give up without a fierce struggle — we are told that Copeland lost his two front teeth in the fight.

A distant view of the city, framed by the Autumn leaves, from the riverside path through Pelaw Wood.

Croxdale Hall has been the residence of the Salvin family – distant relatives of the well-known architect – since the fifteenth century. However much of the present hall was built in the eighteenth century and comprises three ranges around a central courtyard. The nine-acre walled garden is from the seventeenth century and has a terraced walk overlooking two large ponds. The eighteenth century orangery in the centre of the terrace has a long crinkle-crankle wall facing south on either side. The Norman church behind the Hall is not used now but the door has a badly weathered tympanum with a twelfth-century relief panel depicting the Tree of Life. The Hall is open to the public but only by prior arrangement.

Croxdale railway viaduct carries
the main London to Edinburgh line
high above the River Wear.

Brancepeth Castle was originally built by Ralph Neville, the 1st Earl of Westmorland, unfortunately he fell out of favour because of his involvement in the Rising of the North and the estate passed to the Crown. It was eventually granted to Sir Robert Kerr of Ferniehirst – a member of the notorious Border reiver family – but he too fell out of favour when he and his wife were implicated in the poisoning of Sir Thomas Overbury. Eventually the castle came into the ownership of Sir Henry Bellasis whose daughter is remembered as the sweetheart of 'Bonnie Bobbie Shafto' in the famous song. It has, in more recent years, served as the headquarters of the Durham Light Infantry and as a research establishment for Jobling Glassware, manufacturers of the famous 'Pyrex'. It is now in private ownership.

This is the very spot from which St Cuthbert's mist is said to have been seen rising to cover the three towers preventing Durham Cathedral from being bombed during one of the notorious Baedeker Raids by the Luftwaffe in the Second World War.

The Lumiere Festival was a spectacular display of light and music held over four-nights in the city and attracted over 150,000 people. There were over 30 captivating displays by over 50 artists including 'Splash' by Peter Lewis of Canada, which saw Kingsgate Bridge transformed into a colourful waterfall.

The stunning 'Crown of Light' by British artists Ross Ashton, Robert Ziegler and John Del'Nero, involved the projection of images of the Lindisfarne Gospels rolling over Durham Cathedral with a soundtrack of moving and atmospheric music during the Lumiere Festival.

Such was the success of the event that plans are in place to repeat it on a regular basis.